FACTS FANTASTIC

BLACK HOLES

and other space phenomena

Philip Steele

Kingfisher

KINGFISHER
An imprint of Larousse plc
Elsley House, 24-30 Great Titchfield
Street, London, W1P 7AD

First published by Kingfisher 1995
10 9 8 7 6 5 4 3 2
Text copyright © Larousse plc 1995
Illustrations copyright ©
  Larousse plc 1995
Design copyright © David West
  Children's Books 1995

A CIP catalogue record for this book
is available from the British Library

ISBN 1 85697 407 3

Phototypeset from QuarkXPress disk
  by Southern Positives and
  Negatives (SPAN), Lingfield, Surrey
Printed and bound in Hong Kong

Conceived and created by

David West • CHILDREN'S BOOKS

Author: Philip Steele
Consultants: Carole Stott, Ian
  Graham
Cover illustration: Ian Thompson
  and Rob Shone
Illustrations: Ian Thompson
Line illustrations: Rob Shone

CONTENTS

INTRODUCTION

Why are there gigantic black holes in the depths of space? What would happen if a great chunk of space rock smashed into the Earth? When will the Sun stop shining? Why do some stars explode and others fade away? How do astronauts prepare their breakfast on the Space Shuttle?

The more we find out about the fantastic secrets of space, the more questions there are to ask. And this is the book to answer them...

It visits our neighbours, the planets and their moons. It embarks on journeys into deep space, seeking out supernovas and pulsars. And it gives you all the latest information on rockets, satellites and space probes. And there are quizzes that will test you to the limits. Did you know, for example, that in the time you have taken to read this introduction, the light from a star has travelled 18,000,000 kilometres?

CHAPTER ONE

HEAVENLY BODIES

Red giants, white dwarfs, black holes and galaxies... They are all out there, deep in the starry night sky.

But what are they? And what do they look like? Read on, to explore some of the mysteries that are lurking in the dark depths of outer space.

ANCIENT EGYPTIAN and Chinese **astronomers** looked up at the night sky and studied the stars with as much wonder and awe as we do today. But their understanding of space was very different to ours. In fact, it wasn't until 400 years ago that people began to accept that our planet Earth is round. Before this time, most people thought that the world was flat...

The Ancient Egyptians believed the night sky was the body of a goddess called Nut. Her star-spangled body arched over the Earth.

...and that if sailors went on long journeys they were in danger of falling off the edge!

ARISTOTLE, the Ancient Greek thinker, realized that the Earth must be round as early as the 330s BC. He was watching an **eclipse** when he noticed that the Earth was casting a round shadow on the face of the Moon. Aristotle believed that the other planets and the Sun all travel around the Earth.

GALILEO (1564–1642), the great Italian astronomer, studied the sky through the newly-invented **telescope** and came to think that the Earth travels around the Sun, not the Sun around the Earth. This went against the teachings of the Church, and so Galileo was put on trial.

TODAY, people are still arguing about outer space. The most popular theory about the creation of the **universe** is that it began with a vast explosion about 15 **billion** years ago. **Cosmologists** have named this the BIG BANG theory.

After the BIG BANG, the universe kept expanding and is still getting bigger today. Some cosmologists think that the universe will stop expanding and shrink back to nothing in the BIG CRUNCH!

NEW MATTER FORMING

NEW GALAXIES FORMING

OLD GALAXIES

UNIVERSE EXPANDING

THE UNDERSE contains as many as 100 **billion** billion stars, grouped together in gigantic 'star-cities' called **galaxies**. The Big Bang sent the young universe flying out in all directions, and even today the galaxies – and everything in them – are still rushing away from each other at high speed. As the universe grows, galaxies are still forming on its far edges.

THE MILKY WAY

is the name we have given to our own galaxy. It contains about 1,000 billion stars, of which the Sun is just one. We can see it from Earth, as a band of milky-white light across the sky. Out in space, viewed from above, it looks like a gigantic whirlpool with spiralling

The Milky Way (a spiral galaxy) viewed from the side.

arms. Sideways on, it's a bit like two fried eggs stuck together!

Irregular galaxy

Elliptical galaxy

Barred-spiral galaxy

COUNTLESS OTHER GALAXIES lie beyond ours, stretching out into deepest space. Nobody knows exactly how many there are – perhaps as many as 100 billion. Not all of these galaxies are spiral-shaped. Elliptical galaxies are rounded or oval, while irregular galaxies have no special shape at all. Each new galaxy that is discovered is given a number – and sometimes its own name as well. M104 has been nicknamed the Sombrero, because it looks a bit like a big Mexican hat, and the bright, swirling M51 galaxy is known as the Whirlpool!

*Most galaxies are so far away from Earth that they can only be seen through extremely powerful **telescopes**. These telescopes are like giant cameras which take photographs of the sky – **astronomers** do not look through them directly!*

STARS ARE BORN in a great cloud of hydrogen gas and dust called a **nebula**. This begins to break up and shrink into spinning balls. Then each ball becomes so incredibly hot in its centre that **nuclear reactions** are triggered, and the hydrogen starts to turn into another gas called helium. The young star now glows brightly and gives off vast amounts of heat.

1. Our Sun was born in a cold, dark nebula cloud.

2. Stars formed from the nebula.

3. At first the Sun was a cool star.

4. The Sun is now at this stage of its life.

*The Sun might seem huge to us, but it is only a medium-sized star. It has been shining for about 4.6 **billion** years and is about halfway through its life. Its surface is a super-hot cauldron of bubbling gases and great tongues of flame!*

THE BIGGEST stars are called **giants**, and they can have 20 or 30 times as much gas in them as our Sun. They blaze brightly, but soon burn up their gas fuel. Small, dim stars are called **dwarfs**. The brightness of the stars we see from Earth depends on their size and how far away they are from us.

Supergiant

A RED GIANT is an old star which has swollen to many times its normal size. This final blaze of glory happens when the star's helium **core** collapses and gets hot enough to blow its hydrogen up into a vast orange-red ball. The biggest stars may swell into **supergiants**, 2,000 times the size of our Sun.

5. Towards the end of its life, the Sun will swell into a red giant.

Really massive stars – at least eight times the size of the Sun – don't fade slowly. They go out with an almighty bang and look like a bright, new star. Exploding stars are called **supernovas***.*

A WHITE DWARF is almost the final stage in a star's life. The gas surface of the red giant is blown off, and the star is now a planetary nebula. In the centre of the gas shell is the red giant's hot, shrunken core – a white dwarf star. Over billions of years, this fades into a cinder and dies.

6. A planetary nebula

7. A white dwarf

*A black hole would suck in any passing spacecraft within a millionth of a second! Even nearby stars would be gulped up. A giant black hole may lurk at the centre of our own **galaxy**, the Milky Way.*

BLACK HOLES are one of the greatest mysteries of space. We cannot see them, and **astronomers** only know they exist because of their effect on nearby stars. They happen sometimes after a star blows up in a **supernova**. The star's **gravity** pulls all the material that remains after the explosion inwards, squeezing it smaller and smaller. Either a tiny **neutron star** forms or a black hole – an object with such strong gravity that nothing can escape from it, not even light.

PULSARS are neutron stars that spin round and round, giving off a narrow beam of light and radio waves which sweeps through space like a lighthouse beacon. When these rapid pulses of energy were first detected in 1967, astronomers were baffled. Some thought they were hearing messages from aliens!

TWIN STARS are called binaries. These stars spend their lives **orbiting** each other, held together by the pull of each other's gravity. Although the two stars were probably born at the same time, they are often completely different in colour and brightness. Around a quarter of the stars in our galaxy are binaries.

COMETS are giant snowballs made of snow and dust. They **orbit** the Sun, but only a few ever come close to it. If they do, the heat starts to melt them and they grow long tails of gas and dust.

MILLIONS OF ASTEROIDS

orbit the Sun in a belt between the planets Mars and Jupiter. Asteroids are minor planets that come in many different sizes. Many are no larger than a house, but there is a huge asteroid called Ceres which measures around 930 kilometres across.

Some people think that the dinosaurs died out after a huge meteorite hit the Earth, sending up a cloud of dust that blocked out the Sun and fatally changed the climate.

SHOOTING STARS

or **meteors** are light trails created by tiny space rocks burning up as they speed towards the Earth. Larger pieces that survive to crash into the ground are called **meteorites**. No one is known to have been seriously hurt by a meteorite, but an American had a close shave in 1993 – he returned to his car to find that a meteorite had smashed a hole right through it!

The **Facts Fantastic** Quiz

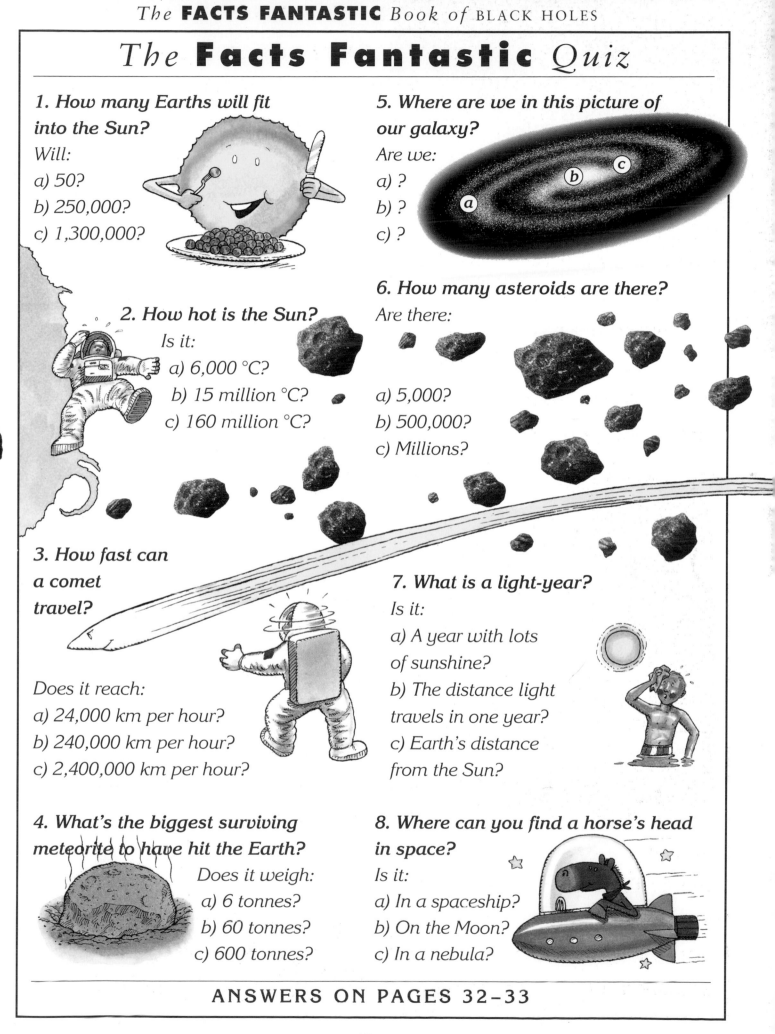

1. How many Earths will fit into the Sun?

Will:

a) 50?

b) 250,000?

c) 1,300,000?

2. How hot is the Sun?

Is it:

a) 6,000 °C?

b) 15 million °C?

c) 160 million °C?

3. How fast can a comet travel?

Does it reach:

a) 24,000 km per hour?

b) 240,000 km per hour?

c) 2,400,000 km per hour?

4. What's the biggest surviving meteorite to have hit the Earth?

Does it weigh:

a) 6 tonnes?

b) 60 tonnes?

c) 600 tonnes?

5. Where are we in this picture of our galaxy?

Are we:

a) ?

b) ?

c) ?

6. How many asteroids are there?

Are there:

a) 5,000?

b) 500,000?

c) Millions?

7. What is a light-year?

Is it:

a) A year with lots of sunshine?

b) The distance light travels in one year?

c) Earth's distance from the Sun?

8. Where can you find a horse's head in space?

Is it:

a) In a spaceship?

b) On the Moon?

c) In a nebula?

ANSWERS ON PAGES 32–33

CHAPTER TWO

OUR FAMILY OF PLANETS

Gigantic volcanoes,
red deserts, yellow skies,
lonely moons...
Our neighbours, the eight
planets, are strange and
mysterious worlds –
observed by space probes,
but not yet explored.

Why do the planets travel
around our star, the Sun?
When were they born?
Could people live on any
planet other than Earth?

THE SOLAR SYSTEM is the name given to the Sun and all the space bodies that move around it – from the nine planets and their moons, to **asteroids** and **comets**. These space bodies are all held in their orbits by the enormous pull of the Sun's **gravity**. Without this, everything would spin away into outer space.

11

8

10

KEY
1. Sun
2. Mercury
3. Venus
4. Earth
5. Mars
6. Asteroid belt
7. Jupiter
8. Saturn
9. Uranus
10. Neptune
11. Pluto

THE PLANETS formed from the leftovers of the **nebula** that gave birth to the Sun. They aren't as big or hot as stars, and they cannot make light of their own. They reflect the Sun's light.

1

2

3

4

5

6

7

9

PLANETS SPIN LIKE TOPS

as they **orbit** the Sun. The time a planet takes to spin around once on its **axis** is called its period of rotation. The time it takes to travel around the Sun is its orbital period. As the planets move through space, most are orbited in turn – by spinning moons.

Axis

Some time after the Sun was born, a huge, spinning doughnut-shaped cloud of gas and dust took shape around it. The dust clumped together, forming the rocky planets. From the gas came the four giant gas planets.

15

MERCURY has been battered and bashed by so many **asteroids**, **comets** and **meteorites** that its surface is scarred with craters. This small planet is the closest to the Sun, and every day there is a heat wave, with temperatures soaring as high as 430 °C. Mercury hasn't enough **atmosphere** to hold in heat, so nights drop to −180 °C, about three times as cold as the lowest temperature recorded on Earth. Mercury rotates slowly – once every 58 Earth-days 16 hours.

VENUS was the goddess of love in Ancient Rome, but the planet named after her is far from lovely. Poisonous yellow clouds blanket its rocky surface, trapping the Sun's heat and making Venus the hottest planet – its temperature reaches 480 °C. Acid rain falls from the clouds and lightning flickers between them. There may also be active volcanoes in its high mountain ranges.

Lightning flickers across Venus' murky, yellow sky.

OUR HOME PLANET,

Earth, has sparkling blue oceans and is wreathed in white clouds. It is the only planet to have oxygen (the gas that all animals need to breathe to stay alive) in its atmosphere. And it is just the right distance from the Sun for it to be neither too hot nor too cold to support an amazing variety of plant and animal life.

OUR MOON is an airless ball of rock. The Sun

lights only one half at a time – the other half is in darkness. And because the Moon only spins once on its **axis** in the 27 Earth-days 7 hours it takes to travel around the Earth, we always see the same face. The Moon appears to change its shape during its **orbit** because we see different parts of its sunlit half at different times.

Wide plains, craters and high mountain ranges make shadowy patterns on the face of the Moon. People often think the patterns look like a face – thus the stories about the Man in the Moon!

New moon

Crescent

First quarter

Gibbous moon

Full moon

Mars

Jupiter has a spotty face! **Telescopes** *show a strange marking called the Great Red Spot, so big that two Earths could fit inside. It is a gigantic hurricane which has been raging for at least 300 years.*

Jupiter

Europa (one of Jupiter's moons)

MARS is only half the size of the Earth. Imagine a desert world covered in red rocks and dunes, under a pink, dusty sky. One of Mars' volcanoes, Olympus Mons,

Ganymede (Jupiter's largest moon)

is the tallest in the **solar system** (three times as high as Mount Everest), while the planet is seamed by huge gorges – also far bigger than any on Earth. These make patterns on the surface of Mars which can be seen from Earth. Some **astronomers** used to think that the gorges were canal-like structures, built by Martians. But **space probes** have yet to find any sign of life there!

JUPITER is the biggest planet in the **solar system**. It is 11 times the size of Earth and contains over 300 times as much material. At its centre is a small, rocky **core**, but the bulk of the planet is made up of hydrogen. Violent storm clouds swirl through its **atmosphere**, which is streaked by flashes of lightning. Jupiter may be a giant, but it is still the fastest spinner of all the planets, rotating once every 9 Earth-hours 55 minutes.

Saturn

The other three gas giants also have rings, but Saturn's are the brightest and most spectacular. They are made up of pieces of rock, ice and dust.

SATURN has the most moons – 18 at the last count – and many people think that its broad, glistening rings make it the most beautiful planet. Like its neighbour Jupiter, Saturn is a gas giant, with a small, rocky core surrounded by hydrogen. It, too, has terrible storms and high winds. Although Saturn is the second largest planet, it is so light that it would actually float in water!

URANUS was the first planet to be discovered with a **telescope** – in 1781. **Space probes** have shown us that it has 11 narrow rings, and 15 moons. Its **atmosphere** is a blue-green blanket of methane gas, with an ocean of hydrogen and a rocky **core** beneath it.

*Uranus has flipped! Most planets have a slightly tilted **axis**, but Uranus is on its side. At some point it must have been tipped over – perhaps by a large **asteroid**.*

NEPTUNE is too far away for **astronomers** to see it clearly from Earth, even through powerful telescopes. It was known to have two moons before 1989, when Voyager 2 revealed another six!

Neptune

Uranus

PLUTO is a tiny frozen planet, with a moon called Charon which is half its size. Both are thought to be icy balls of rock and frozen methane. Pluto wasn't discovered until 1930, after years of scientific detective work.

Pluto

The **Facts Fantastic** Quiz

1. Which planet is closest in size to Earth?

Is it:

a) Saturn?

b) Venus?

c) Mars?

2. Which planet is named after the god of war?

Is it:

a) Jupiter?

b) Mercury?

c) Mars?

3. Where is a 'day' longer than a year?

Is it:

a) On Earth?

b) On the Moon?

c) On Venus?

4. Which planet was bombed by a comet in 1994?

Was it:

a) Jupiter?

b) Pluto?

c) Mars?

5. Which moons' names mean 'fear' and 'terror'?

Are they:

a) Titan and Mimas?

b) Io and Ganymede?

c) Phobos and Deimos?

6. Which planet may not really be a planet?

Is it:

a) Jupiter?

b) Neptune?

c) Pluto?

7. Which planet is farthest from the Sun?

Is it:

a) Uranus?

b) Pluto?

c) Neptune?

8. On which planet do winds reach 2,000 km/h?

Is it:

a) Neptune?

b) Saturn?

c) Mercury?

ANSWERS ON PAGES 34–35

CHAPTER THREE

VIKINGS & OTHER VOYAGERS

This century we have embarked on the greatest adventure in our history – the exploration of the solar system!

Rockets, satellites, space probes and stations... How do they work, what missions have they accomplished, and what are their destinations?

THE CHINESE were making firework **rockets** 900 years ago. They were powered by black powder, an early kind of gunpowder. In 1903, a Russian scientist called Konstantin Tsiolkovsky worked out how to use liquid fuels to power rockets.

AN AMERICAN scientist called Robert Goddard launched the first liquid-fuel rocket in 1926. It was nearly 3.5 metres long and it burnt petrol and liquid oxygen. This created a jet of gas which lifted the rocket 12.5 metres.

Goddard and his rocket

SPUTNIK 1 was launched by the USSR on October 4, 1957. It was the first artificial satellite ever to be sent into space. It stayed in orbit for three months before burning up.

Sputnik 1

SPACE ROCKETS were developed in the USA and USSR (now Russia), during the 1950s. At first they were used to launch artificial **satellites** into **orbit** around the Earth. A rocket has to reach a speed of at least 11 kilometres per second before it can escape the pull of Earth's **gravity**. That's 77 times the speed of the world's fastest train!

Yuri Gagarin

Valentina Tereshkova

The first person to walk in space was the cosmonaut (Russian astronaut) Aleksei Leonov, on March 18, 1965. He was outside his spacecraft for 20 minutes.

THE FIRST MAN IN SPACE was Yuri Gagarin, a Russian who orbited the Earth in Vostok 1, on April 12, 1961. The first woman, Valentina Tereshkova, took off in Vostok 6 in 1963.

Command module

Service module

Lunar module

3rd stage rocket

2nd stage rocket

1st stage rocket

USA

THE FIRST SUCCESSFUL MOON LANDING took place on July 20, 1969, when US astronauts Neil Armstrong and Buzz Aldrin became the first people to set foot on the Moon. A huge three-stage Saturn 5 **rocket** had blasted off from Earth four days earlier, carrying a spacecraft which had three sections called modules. While the Command and Service modules **orbited** the Moon, the Lunar Module travelled down to its surface. There were five more Moon landings, during which astronauts carried out experiments and collected rock and soil samples for analysis back on Earth.

A third crew member, Michael Collins, stayed in orbit while the other two travelled down to the Moon's surface.

A US flag flies on the Moon. Or does it? The Moon has no air and therefore no wind. In fact, the flag in the famous pictures was held up by wire!

UNITED STATES

SPACE STATIONS are designed to stay in orbit around the Earth for long periods of time, so that astronauts and cosmonauts can live and work in space. Smaller spacecraft can dock with the station, bringing up fresh crews. Skylab was a US station in orbit from 1973 to 1979. Mir is a Russian station, launched in 1986.

Skylab

Mir space station

Docking port

Solar panels turn sunlight into electricity

Working and living quarters

RETURNING TO EARTH is dangerous.

The **atmosphere** around our planet burns up most objects that travel through it. Capsules containing astronauts are protected by heat shields. Parachutes slow the capsule as it nears the Earth's surface.

One Russian cosmonaut has lived in space for over a year. Things are virtually weightless in space, so they float about unless held down. Long periods of weightlessness can weaken muscles and bones.

THE SPACE SHUTTLE is a US spacecraft which can be reused. It is launched by **rockets**, and then goes into **orbit** around the Earth. When it returns to the ground, it glides down and lands on a runway. The Shuttle Orbiter may be used to release **satellites** into space, or to capture and repair them. Or it may carry a small laboratory called Spacelab in its cargo bay, where crews conduct experiments. Astronauts can use jet-powered backpacks called MMUs to move around outside the craft.

A crew member uses an MMU (manned manoeuvring unit) to space-walk and guide a damaged satellite onto the Shuttle Orbiter's long manipulator arm. The satellite will be pulled into the cargo bay for repair.

3. *The main fuel tank drops away and breaks up on re-entry.*

2a. *The booster rockets fall away.*

1. *The Shuttle takes off, using liquid fuel from a main tank and two solid-fuel booster rockets.*

2b. *The boosters parachute back to Earth, for reuse.*

KEY
a) Flight deck
b) Air lock
c) Manipulator arm
d) Cargo bay
e) Cargo bay doors
f) Crew member with MMU
g) Rescued satellite
h) Landing gear
i) Fuel tanks
j) Main engines
k) Orbiter engines
l) Thrusters for manoeuvring

BURAN is a Russian shuttle which was launched by powerful Energia rockets on November 15, 1988. It was controlled by computers and did not have a crew. Unmanned missions may save lives, but some problems are best solved by people on the spot.

4. The Shuttle Orbiter goes into Earth orbit, cruising at 27,800 km/h.

5. The Orbiter turns around and fires rockets to slow down.

6. The Orbiter manoeuvres into re-entry position.

7. The Orbiter re-enters Earth's atmosphere. Heat-proof tiles prevent it from burning up.

8. The Orbiter glides back towards the landing site.

9. The Orbiter lands on the runway at about 350 km/h.

c

g

f

i

l

k

j

i

k

l

h

Communications satellite

Weather satellite

Landsat

Seasat

ARTIFICIAL SATELLITES have come a long way since the Sputnik days. Communications satellites now bounce radio, television and telephone signals around our planet. Military satellites can spy and guide missiles. Weather satellites track hurricanes and help with forecasting. Other satellites map the land and the oceans, and collect information on the environment. Yet others gaze beyond the **solar system**, to discover the secrets of deep space.

Space is littered with junk! There are bits and pieces of broken satellites, old tools and other rubbish. And that's dangerous. At the speeds reached by the Shuttle, even a speck of paint is a serious hazard.

Hubble Space Telescope

THE HUBBLE SPACE TELESCOPE orbits the Earth at a height of 590 kilometres and gives us unique views of distant parts of the **universe**. When it was first launched in

1990, its 'eyesight' was a bit faulty – the pictures it sent back to Earth were fuzzy. It was repaired in 1993, by astronauts space-walking from the Space Shuttle *Endeavour*. As well as mending or replacing various instruments and controls, the astronauts managed to fit a set of mirrors which work a bit like glasses to correct Hubble's eyesight.

Ulysses

SPACE PROBES can be speeded on their way by using the pull of another planet's **gravity**. The Ulysses probe was launched in 1990 and passed Jupiter in 1992, using its gravity to swing onto a path that took it over the Sun's **poles** in 1994 and 1995.

GIOTTO was launched in 1985 to study Halley's **Comet**, and in 1986 passed within 600 kilometres of its **core**. The space probe was battered by comet dust, but it still sent back images that allowed scientists to work out that the core measured 16 km by 8 km.

In 1992 Giotto investigated the comet Grigg-Skjellerup.

FANTASTIC VOYAGES of discovery have been carried out by unmanned **space probes**. Russian Venera probes parachuted down to the surface of Venus in the 1960s to 1980s, and managed to send back pictures before being destroyed by the planet's **atmosphere**. Back in 1976, the USA's two Viking probes dropped landers on Mars. The USA's Cassini probe is to be launched towards Saturn in the late 1990s. It will drop a mini-probe by parachute to study the atmosphere of Saturn's largest moon, Titan.

Viking space probe

Voyager 2 photographs Saturn

FLY-BY PROBES zip around the planets, taking pictures as they pass. The USA's Mariners spied on Venus, Mars and Mercury in the 1960s and 1970s. But the superstars have been Pioneer 10 and 11, and Voyager 1 and 2. Since their launch in the 1970s, a torrent of priceless information has poured back to us on Earth.

Will we ever live on another planet? Both the USA and Russia have plans for human settlements on Mars – but space probes are expected to pave the way, by dropping an army of robot explorers.

Mariner 10 over Mercury

The **Facts Fantastic** Quiz

1. Who has got a message for aliens?

Is it:

a) The postman?

b) The Space Shuttle?

c) The Pioneer probes?

2. Who sent messages from Mars?

Was it:

a) A Martian?

b) A Viking?

c) A Norman?

3. What keeps satellites in orbit?

Is it:

a) Rockets?

b) Solar panels?

c) Earth's gravity?

4. Who spies from space?

Is it:

a) Satellites?

b) Spies in spacesuits?

c) Aliens?

5. What happened to Skylab?

Did it:

a) Fly off into space?

b) Crash back to Earth?

c) Land safely on Earth?

6. How do astronauts go to the toilet?

Do they:

a) Wait until they return to Earth?

b) Use a special toilet?

c) Use a normal toilet?

7. How do astronauts prepare their food?

Do they:

a) Use an oven?

b) Eat cold food?

c) Go on a diet?

8. Where is the space probe Voyager 1 now?

Is it:

a) On Pluto?

b) In deep space?

c) In a museum?

ANSWERS ON PAGES 36–37

The **Answers** to Chapter One (PAGE 13)

1. How many Earths will fit into the Sun?

Answer: c)

The Sun looks small from Earth, but that's because it is so far away – about 150 million km!

The Sun is vast, of course. Its diameter is nearly 1.4 million km – 109 times that of Earth. Well over a million Earths could fit inside it.

2. How hot is the Sun?

Answer: a) and b)

The Sun's heat is generated by **nuclear reactions** in its superhot **core**. The temperature there reaches a staggering 15 million °C. It can take as long as a million years for this heat to move up through the Sun's layers to its surface, the photosphere, where the temperature is about 6,000 °C – this is still hot enough to make solid iron bars boil away into clouds of gas!

3. How fast can a comet travel?

Answer: b)

All **comets** travel at different speeds, and they are fastest when their **orbits** bring them close to the Sun. Halley's Comet averages 240,000 km/h. No comet reaches speeds greater than 2,376,000 km/h.

PHOTOSPHERE

CONVECTIVE LAYER

RADIATIVE LAYER

CORE

4. What's the biggest surviving meteorite to have hit the Earth?

Answer: b)

The largest known **meteorite** lies where it fell to Earth thousands of years ago – at Hoba West in Namibia, Africa. It weighs a massive 60 tonnes. Meteor Crater, in the US state of Arizona, is 170 metres deep and was probably created by a meteorite about 45 metres wide.

5. Where are we in this picture of our galaxy?

Answer: a)
Just in case you get lost in outer space – we live on one of the Milky Way's spiralling arms, about 28,000 light-years from the centre! From one side to the other, our **galaxy** measures about 100,000 light-years. It looks like a giant Catherine wheel.

6 How many asteroids are there?

Answer: a) and c)
There are millions of chunks of rock in the **asteroid** belt between Mars and Jupiter. Just over 5,000 have been named. There are also other, smaller asteroid groups which follow different orbits.

7. What is a light-year?

Answer: b)
A light-year is the distance a ray of light travels through space in one year. Light travels at about 300,000 km per second, and a light-year is around 9.46 million million km. When we look at a star that is 100 light-years away, we are seeing it as it was 100 years ago – the time its light has taken to reach us.

8. Where can you find a horse's head in space?

Answer: c)
The Horsehead **Nebula** is in the star-group of Orion. The horse's head is a dark cloud of cool gas and dust, which stands out against the bright light of newly-formed stars beyond it.

The **Answers** to Chapter Two (PAGE 21)

1. Which planet is closest in size to Earth?

Answer: b)
Check the planet facts on these pages and you will see that it's Venus, which is also our nearest neighbour. Differences between us include the fact that Venus spins in a clockwise direction – the opposite way to Earth.

KEY
Planet's name
Distance from Sun
Diameter
Number of moons
Period of rotation
Orbital period

Mercury
58 million km
4,878 km
0
58 days 16 hrs
88 days

Venus
108 million km
12,102 km
0
243 days 14 min
225 days

2. Which planet is named after the god of war?

Answer: c)
Mars was the name the Romans gave to their god of war. The planet was named after him because its red glow in the night sky reminded people of blood. All the planets, except our own Earth, are named after Greek or Roman gods and goddesses.

3. Where is a 'day' longer than a year?

Answer: c)
Venusians – if there were any – would celebrate their first birthday before they were one day old! Venus takes longer to spin around once than it does to **orbit** the Sun. Its period of rotation is 243 Earth-days. Its orbital period, or 'year', is a fraction under 225 Earth-days.

Orbital period —
Sun
Period of rotation —

Earth
150 million km
12,756 km
1
23 hrs 56 min
365 days

Mars
228 million km
6,786 km
2
24 hrs 37 min
687 days

Jupiter
778 million km
142,984 km
16
9 hrs 55 min
11.9 years

Venus
Goddess of
Love

Jupiter
King of
the gods

Uranus
God of the
Heavens

Pluto God of the
Underworld

Mercury
Messenger of
the gods

Mars
God of
War

Saturn
God of
Farming

Neptune
God of
the Sea

4. Which planet was bombed by a comet in 1994?

Answer: a)

Jupiter's **gravity** *sucked in a passing* **comet** *called Shoemaker-Levy, which then broke up into huge chunks. The collisions were spectacular as these punched into Jupiter's* **atmosphere**.

6. Which planet may not really be a planet?

Answer: c)

Pluto was called a planet when it was discovered in 1930, but some **astronomers** *are beginning to wonder... Pluto is more like a moon than a planet, and it is strange to find a rocky planet so far from the Sun – Pluto's neighbours are the four gas giants.*

Pluto
5,914 million km
2,284 km
1
6 days 9 hrs
248.5 years

Neptune
4,497 million km
49,528 km
8
19 hrs 12 min
164.8 years

Uranus
2,871 million km
51,118 km
15
17 hrs 54 min
84 years

Saturn
1,427 million km
120,536 km
18
10 hrs 40 min
29.5 years

5. Which moons' names mean 'fear' and 'terror'?

Answer: c)

Do you speak Ancient Greek? No? Well, Phobos means 'fear' and Deimos means 'terror' in Greek. They are those little potato-shaped moons that spin around Mars – tiny worlds of cratered and scarred black rock.

Neptune

Sun

7. Which planet is farthest from the Sun?

Answer: b) and c)

Between 1979 and 1999 (and for 20 years of every 248.5-year orbit), Pluto is closer to the Sun than Neptune.

Pluto

8. On which planet do winds reach 2,000 km/h?

Answer: a)

Neptune is the windiest planet.

The **Answers** to Chapter Three (PAGE 31)

1. Who has got a message for aliens?
Answer: c)

A special picture was fixed to the **probes** Pioneer 10 and 11 before they started their long trek through the **solar system**. It showed a man and a woman, and a diagram giving Earth's position in the solar system – just in case there are any alien beings out there who might find it...

2. Who sent messages from Mars?
Answer: b)

Two Viking landers were sent down to the surface of Mars in 1976. Between them, they sent back 3,000 images as well as measuring wind speed and temperature, and carrying out tests on Martian soil. But they didn't find any signs of life!

A Viking lander

3. What keeps satellites in orbit?
Answer: c)

Once a **satellite** has been launched into **orbit** by a **rocket** or Space Shuttle,

Gyroscopes check the satellite is the right way up.

Gas thrusters keep the satellite on course.

it is held in position by Earth's **gravity**. However, power is still needed to control the height, course and speed of the satellite's orbit. Gas thrusters (controlled by computer from Earth) are used to manoeuvre it, while gyroscopes monitor its balance and solar panels provide electrical power.

Solar panels convert the Sun's energy into electrical power.

4. Who spies from space?

Answer: a)

A hundred years ago, armies sent up spies in hot-air balloons to draw pictures of the enemy's position and weapons. Today, special spy satellites are sent into orbit. These can photograph movements of troops, tanks or rocket-launchers – every detail of enemy activity. Spy satellites have sharp enough 'eyesight' to see car number plates!

Geostationary orbit

5. What happened to Skylab?

Answer: b)

On July 11, 1979, the US space station Skylab re-entered Earth's **atmosphere**. It burned up over the Indian Ocean and pieces of it rained down over the West Australian coast – fortunately nobody was hurt – not even a kangaroo!

6. How do astronauts go to the toilet?

Answer: b)

The first astronauts wore collecting bags, but Mir and the Space Shuttle have special toilets. The toilets are quite comfortable, but weightlessness means that astronauts have to pull a bar across their legs to stop themselves floating off the seat. A flow of air sucks away the waste, which is dried.

7. How do astronauts prepare their food?

Answer: a) and b)

Space meals are precooked and packaged in sealed containers. They can be eaten cold or warmed in an oven. Drinks are sucked through a special straw.

8. Where is the space probe Voyager 1 now?

Answer: b)

All the Pioneer and Voyager space probes have now left the solar system and are heading out into deep space. Pioneer 10 is the farthest from home.

USEFUL WORDS

ASTEROID *One of the millions of small rocky bodies orbiting the Sun. More than 90 percent of asteroids are found between Mars and Jupiter.*

ASTRONOMER *Someone who studies the stars and other heavenly bodies.*

ATMOSPHERE *The layer of gases around a planet (its 'air'), which is held down by gravity. Earth's atmosphere is mainly nitrogen and oxygen gas. Smaller bodies with weak gravity, such as the Moon, have no atmosphere.*

AXIS *The imaginary line through the centre of a star, planet or moon, around which it spins.*

BILLION *One thousand million (1,000,000,000).*

BLACK HOLE *A space object with such strong gravity that nothing can escape from it, not even light.*

COMET *One of billions of balls of snow and dust (kilometres in diameter) that orbit the Sun.*

CORE *The centre of a planet or star.*

COSMOLOGIST *Somebody who studies the universe – how it began, its history, and what may happen to it.*

DWARF STAR *Either an ordinary, small, dim star, or the dying remains of a bright star (white or brown dwarf).*

ECLIPSE *There are two kinds of eclipse. An eclipse of the Sun happens if the Moon's orbit takes it directly between the Earth and the Sun. An eclipse of the Moon takes place if the full moon passes directly through the Earth's shadow. The Moon turns a reddish-brown colour.*

GALAXY *A vast number of stars held together by gravity.*

GIANT STAR *Either a star that is hotter and brighter than our Sun (white or blue giant), or an old star that has begun to expand and cool when it has used up its hydrogen fuel (red giant).*

GRAVITY *Every object in the universe has this pulling force. The larger the object, the stronger its gravity. The Earth's gravity keeps our feet on the ground and stops us floating into space, while the Sun's much stronger gravity holds the Earth in orbit around it.*

METEOR *The streak of light seen when a meteoroid (a small piece of space rock) burns up in the Earth's atmosphere.*

METEORITE *A meteoroid (see METEOR) that hits the ground because it is too big to burn up.*

NEBULA *A huge cloud of gas and dust in a galaxy. Stars are born inside nebulae.*

NEUTRON STAR *The hot ball of solid material which is all that remains after a giant star explodes in a supernova.*

NUCLEAR REACTION *All substances are made up of invisibly tiny atoms, and the nucleus at the centre of each atom contains huge amounts of energy. A nuclear reaction is when the nucleus of an atom is changed in some way (by the heat inside a star, for example), releasing some of its energy as heat and light.*

ORBIT *The curved path of something that travels around a star or planet. Each planet, including Earth, has its own orbit around the Sun.*

POLES *The two opposite points on the surface of a spinning star, planet or moon, where the axis passes through it.*

ROCKET *A machine that burns fuel to produce hot gases. As the gases shoot out backwards, they thrust the rocket forwards or upwards at great speed. Space rockets carry tanks of liquid fuel (often hydrogen) and oxygen. (Oxygen is needed because things will not burn without it.)*

SATELLITE *Anything that orbits a planet. Moons are natural satellites. Artificial (man-made) satellites are spacecraft that orbit the Earth.*

SOLAR SYSTEM *Our Sun, and the comets, asteroids, nine planets and their moons that orbit it.*

SPACE PROBE *A crewless spacecraft which leaves the Earth's orbit to explore other planets and moons, comets and asteroids.*

SUPERGIANT *A really massive star, hundreds of times bigger than our Sun.*

SUPERNOVA *A colossal explosion which destroys a giant star. A neutron star or a black hole may be all that is left after a supernova.*

TELESCOPE *An instrument for studying distant objects, such as planets or stars. Optical telescopes work by gathering the light from distant objects, and focussing it through lenses and by mirrors. Radio telescopes have huge dishes which collect radio signals given off by distant space bodies.*

UNIVERSE *The whole of space and everything it contains.*

INDEX